P9-ELX-412
3 2175 00767 5673

READING POWER

Helping Organizations

The Red Cross

Anastasia Suen

The Rosen Publishing Group's
PowerKids Press™
New York

Published in 2002 by The Rosen Publishing Group, Inc.
29 East 21st Street, New York, NY 10010

First Edition

Book Design: Michelle Innes

Photo Credits: © The Red Cross

Suen, Anastasia.
The Red Cross / by Anastasia Suen.
    p. cm. — (Helping organizations)
Includes bibliographical references and index.
ISBN 0-8239-6003-X (library binding)
1. Red Cross—Juvenile literature. 2. American Red Cross—Juvenile literature. 3. Disaster relief—Juvenile literature. 4. Disaster relief—United States—Juvenile literature. I. Title.
HV568 .S79 2001
361.7'7—dc21
                                                    2001000281

Manufactured in the United States of America

Contents

mon keu

The Red Cross

In 1859, Henry Dunant saw people injured in a battle in Italy. He wanted to try to help all people hurt in wars. He told many people about his idea. In 1864, the International Red Cross was started.

In 1881, Clara Barton started the American Red Cross. She wanted to help people in times of war and peace.

Clara Barton was called "the Angel of the Battlefield."

5

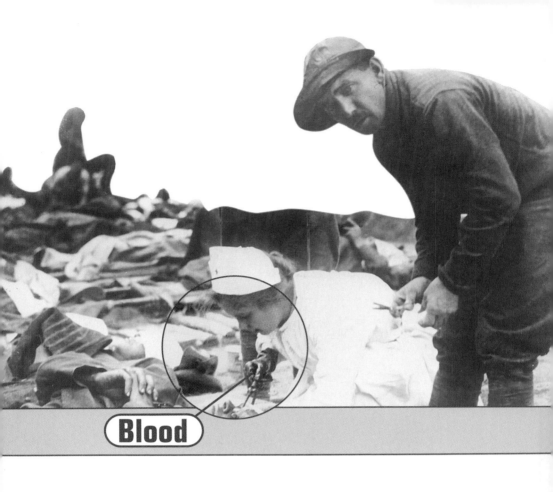

Blood

Red Cross volunteers have helped
in many wars. In World War I,
18,000 nurses joined the American
Red Cross.

During World War II, the Red Cross sent blood to the soldiers. This saved many lives.

Blood

In the 1920s and 1930s, Red Cross nurses worked hard to fight against childhood diseases in the United States. They checked children to help them stay healthy.

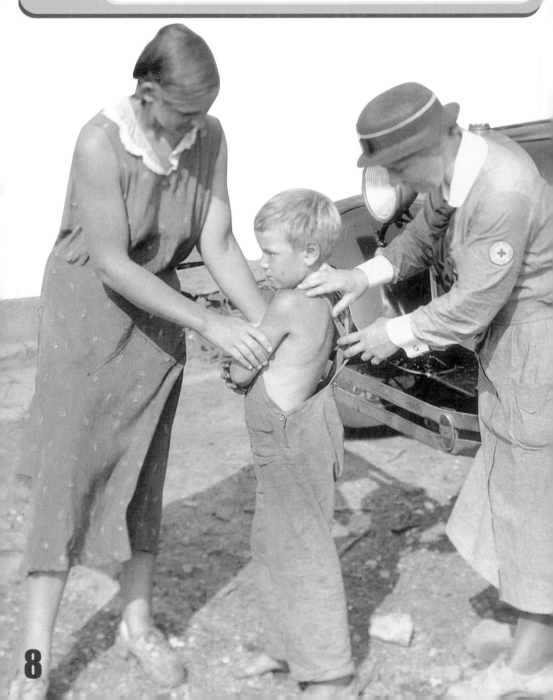

American Red Cross volunteers help in times of peace, too. Volunteers work all over the United States to help those in need. The Red Cross helps anywhere it is needed.

Emergencies

The Red Cross has helped when there are floods, fires, tornadoes, hurricanes, and many other kinds of emergencies.

It's a Fact

The Red Cross
helps 150 families
a day who lose
their homes to fire.

11

A Red Cross volunteer gives food to some children after an earthquake in California.

When there is an emergency, Red Cross volunteers bring food, clothing, and medicine. Volunteers also help by setting up shelters for people who have lost their homes.

Volunteers

Almost all of the people who work for the Red Cross are volunteers. Many people give their time, their money, and even their blood to the Red Cross.

It's a Fact

1 in 200 Americans is a Red Cross volunteer.

Growing Number of
Red Cross Volunteers

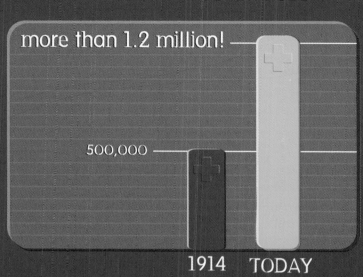

more than 1.2 million!

500,000

1914   TODAY

15

Blood from the Red Cross is used in more than 3,000 hospitals every year.

The American Red Cross gets about six million pints of blood each year.

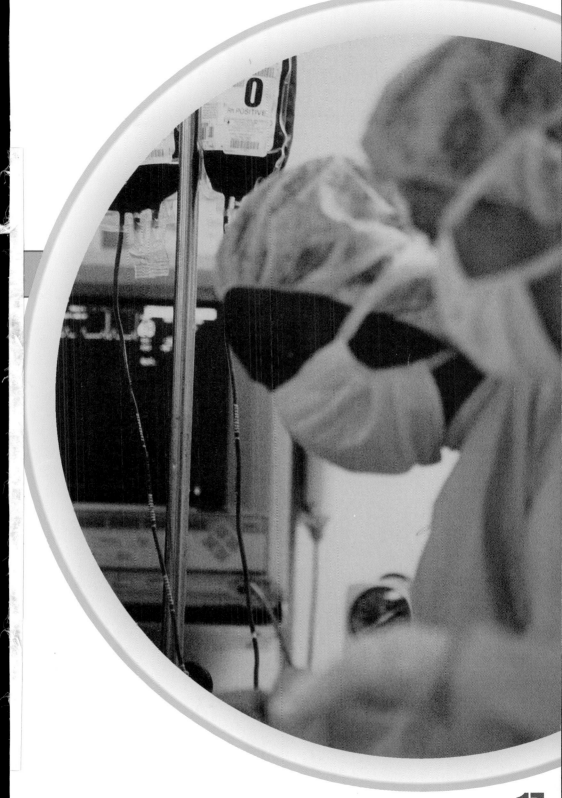

Many volunteers teach first-aid classes. First-aid classes show people how to help themselves and save others.

Some first-aid classes show what to do when someone has stopped breathing.

It's a Fact

15 million
Americans take
classes with the
Red Cross.

The American Red
Cross at Work

The Red Cross helps millions of
people all over the world each year.
If you want to help the Red Cross,
call the Red Cross group near you.

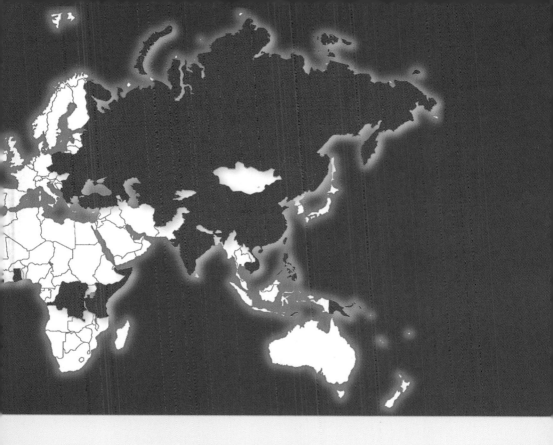

It's a Fact

The American Red
Cross is at work in
more than 100
countries.

Glossary

battle (**bat**-l) a fight between armies

emergencies (ih-**mer**-juhn-seez) situations that call for action right away

international (ihn-tuhr-**nash**-uh-nuhl) between two or more countries

shelter (**shehl**-tuhr) protection from weather, danger, or attack

volunteer (vahl-uhn-**tihr**) someone who works without pay

Resources

Books

Clara Barton
by David Collins
Barbour Publishing, Inc. (1999)

The Red Cross and The Red Crescent
by Michael Pollard
Silver Burdett Press (1994)

Web Site
http://www.redcross.org/services/youth

Index

Word Count: 258

Note to Librarians, Teachers, and Parents

If reading is a challenge, Reading Power is a solution! Reading Power is perfect for readers who want high-interest subject matter at an accessible reading level. These fact-filled, photo-illustrated books are designed for readers who want straightforward vocabulary, engaging topics, and a manageable reading experience. With clear picture/text correspondence, leveled Reading Power books put the reader in charge. Now readers have the power to get the information they want and the skills they need in a user-friendly format.